D1607699

'THE MUSICAL PILGRIM'

General Editor   Dr. Arthur Somervell

BOOKS I-II

MOZART'S
STRING QUARTETS

BY

THOMAS F. DUNHILL

BOOK I

GREENWOOD PRESS, PUBLISHERS
WESTPORT, CONNECTICUT

Originally published in 1927
by Oxford University Press, London

Reprinted from an original copy in the collections
of the Brooklyn Public Library

First Greenwood Reprinting 1970

Library of Congress Catalogue Card Number 77-104260

SBN 8371-3919-8

Printed in the United States of America

CONTENTS

BOOK I

INTRODUCTION . . . 5

I. THE EARLY STRING QUARTETS . . 11

II. THE SIX STRING QUARTETS DEDICATED TO
HAYDN . . . 26

Quartet in G (K. 387) . . 28

Quartet in D minor (K. 421) . 35

Quartet in E flat (K. 428) . . 43

BOOK I

Introduction

MOZART, it is reported, was described by Hans von Bülow, fifty years ago or so, as a young composer with a great future before him. Von Bülow was something of a musical seer as well as a humorist, and his prophecy has been abundantly fulfilled.

Unlike most young composers, Mozart has retained his youth and his appeal to youth. In these days, when we find Beethoven's chamber works most unjustly and ridiculously attacked for their ' pretentious emptiness ' and worse, it is at least comforting to find a general consensus of opinion that the compositions of his immediate predecessor are possessed of an unassailable beauty. Mozart, happily, seems to appeal to the devotees of all schools of musical thought. The classically minded have never lost him : the ultra-modernists, led into the way of truth by Sir Thomas Beecham and other disciples, have rediscovered him and now hold the faith with astonishing unity of spirit. Changes of fashion, which are very frequent in other directions, seem powerless to dethrone the beloved Mozart from the affections of either our Tories or our Bolsheviks.

How much of this devotion is due to the fact that there is a strong reaction against music which is heavily charged with romanticism it is difficult to say. There is a certain impersonal quality in the pre-Beethoven classics which appeals to almost every type of musical mind. We may dwell upon the different characteristics of Haydn and Mozart. We may recognize that, though both composers were high-spirited, where Haydn was exuberant Mozart was volatile, where Haydn was humorous in a blunt or obvious way Mozart was witty in a subtle way, and so on. But the similarities are far greater than the differences. The musical outlook of these two great masters is far more alike than that of any two great masters of the present day. It is perhaps because Mozart gives us the most perfect expression of the outlook of his time that we treasure his music so highly.

E. J. Dent, in his admirable treatise on Mozart's operas,[1] makes a very interesting general observation. ' When we hear the music of a composer whose mode of expression is so remote from our own as is Mozart's,' he says, ' we inevitably tend to fasten on the externals of his music in the belief that they are his most vital characteristics.' Further, he adds that ' most of those features of Mozart's music which we are apt to consider so typically Mozartian are not Mozartian in the least, but are simply the common stock-in-trade of all the music-makers of the day '.

This is very true. If we are searching for individuality in music we shall find the period of Haydn and Mozart a hunting-ground upon which we are likely to stumble. We should certainly remember that individuality of style means far more to us than it meant to musicians of Mozart's day.

It is not until the older classical type of music was superseded by the romantic that much importance was attached to the personality of a composer. We are apt to value a piece of music for what we regard as its exceptional, its unique qualities—for its freedom in self-expression. But in the eighteenth century the

[1] E. J. Dent, *Mozart's Operas*, Chatto & Windus.

great composers were looked upon as the guardians of traditions. They accepted the trust, and respected, even reverenced, the limitations of art as then defined. They were, indeed, proud to conform to a standard of aesthetic morality that we moderns neither recognize nor understand. It was Beethoven, the conscious revolutionary in music, who cast these ideas to the winds and first made a virtue of individuality. And so a new school of thought arose which magnified the personal, the egoistic, and dominating element, and thereby lost a good deal of the purity and serenity which made the work of the older masters so general and universal.

Of recent years the aggrandizement of personality has been so dominating and so shameless that it is not surprising to find people returning with ever-increasing affection to the work of a composer who, as Ernest Newman has said, ' never wrote a page that does not touch the spiritual ear with a caress '. Mozart's music is ' of humanity yet above humanity : it is the pure soul of man purged of all the grossness of his clay '.

Such a composer as this was in his true element in chamber music. The spirituality that was in him did not demand big forces for its expression. The less mechanism he employed, the more he was able to touch us. Therefore in the string quartet—the most intimate and expressive of combinations, where a strong volume of sound is impossible and the purity of the musical idea is everything—he was most truly great.

Mozart wrote twenty-three string quartets, not counting the three Divertimenti or the Serenade (' Kleine Nachtmusik '), which were probably intended for string orchestra, or the Adagio and Fugue, dealt with in the second part of this book. Only about six of these works are at all familiar to the public—five of the set dedicated to Haydn and the isolated example in D major written in 1786. In this matter it cannot be urged that popular opinion has gone astray, for these well-known examples are unquestionably Mozart's greatest masterpieces in this field. At the same time the student will find the earliest quartets, written between 1770 and 1773, of great interest in view of the hints they give of what was to come, and no apology is needed for the consideration which is bestowed upon such little-known works in these pages. It is even more desirable that his attention should be directed to the three unfamiliar quartets of Mozart's last years : it is true that they were written to order and were in some respects perfunctory, but mastery is shown in the presentation of some remarkable new methods, and the musical speech is as beautiful as ever, even if the thoughts which that speech expresses seem to spring no longer from the heart.

This book should be read, if possible, with the scores of the quartets at hand. It is hoped, however, that the plentiful use of examples in music type will render its perusal easier and more intelligible. A good many of the scores are unfortunately not available in cheap form, but miniature copies of the six quartets dedicated to Haydn are procurable for about a shilling apiece in the Eulenberg Edition from Messrs. Goodwin & Tabb (Kammermusik, Nos. 1, 32, 33, 34, 35, and 8), and also those of the popular D major Quartet and the three final quartets (Kammermusik, Nos. 24, 25, 26, and 27). The only complete edition of the works discussed in this book is that published by Breitkopf & Härtel with the co-operation of Dr. Ludwig Köchel. The scores of all Mozart's string quartets are to be found in Series 14 of this monumental collection. Mozart's compositions are so numerous that they can only be readily identified by what are always known as the Köchel numbers. These numbers are given throughout this book in connexion with each work mentioned, preceded by the letter K.

Lastly, the great value of the gramophone as an aid to the study of chamber music should not be overlooked. Several excellent performances of Mozart's finest string quartets have been successfully recorded. The author has taken pains to ascertain particulars of these, which will be found tabulated on another page.

T. F. D.

London, 1926.

Gramophone Records
of Mozart's String Quartets.

'Columbia' Records.

Record Nos.	Work.	Players.
L. 1606–8	Quartet in B flat (K. 458) (complete)	Léner String Quartet
L. 1520	Quartet in D minor (K. 421) (*Allegretto ma non troppo* only)	"
D. 1427	Quartet in D minor (K. 421) (*Allegro moderato* and *Andante*)	London String Quartet
L. 1043–4	Quartet in E flat (K. 428) (all movements : some cuts probable)	"
L. 1545–8	Quartet in C (K. 465) (complete)	Léner String Quartet
L. 1530	Quartet in G (K. 387) (*Andante cantabile* only)	"

'His Master's Voice' Records.

DB. 249	Quartet in D (K. 575) (*Andante* only)	Flonzaley Quartet
DB. 254	Quartet in D (K. 575) (*Minuet* only)	"
DB. 251	Quartet in D minor (K. 421) (*Finale* only)	"
DA. 174	Quartet in D minor (K. 421) (*Minuet* only)	Elman String Quartet
DB. 238	Quartet in E flat (K. 428) (*Minuet* only)	"
DB. 252	Quartet in G (K. 387) (*Finale* only)	Flonzaley Quartet

'Vocalion' Records.

K. 05190–3	Quartet in D minor (K. 421) (complete)	Kutcher String Quartet
D. 02013–4	Quartet in D (K. 575) (all movements : some cuts probable)	London String Quartet

I

The Early String Quartets

MOZART's first string quartet (K. 80) (with the exception of a Rondo finale, added at some later time) was composed in 1770 at Lodi, during his first journey to Italy. The composer was then only fourteen years of age.

It begins with an Adagio in G major of considerable proportions, which is followed by a very short Allegro in the same key—a sonatina movement rather than a sonata movement—and a Minuet, also in G, with a Trio in C. The opening theme of the Adagio is exceedingly graceful, and already characteristically Mozartian in its turn of phrase.

Ex. 1.

No marked thematic originality is forthcoming, but there are some quite skilful points of elaboration, evidently accomplished with childish delight.

It is interesting to observe that the 2nd violin is treated with much freedom and independence, and is frequently employed to execute passages quite as enterprising as those allotted to the leader. The lower parts, especially that of the 'cello, are less confidently dealt with, and contrapuntal movement is generally confined to the two violins. The Rondo, alluded to above, is not only more decisive in style than the foregoing movements, but far better balanced in form and more delicate in texture, which seems to point to its being the product of a considerably later period.

The three quartets called Divertimenti (K. 136–8), which are each in three movements and do not differ much in design from the other quartets of his earlier years, appear to come next in chronological order. They were composed in 1772 and are rhythmical and precise in manner, without, however, possessing any very striking features.

A little later, on his journey to Milan in October of the same year and during his sojourn there, Mozart busied himself with the writing of further string quartets. There are six in this group (K. 155–60), and all clearly belong to the same period. Each of these quartets comprises three movements only. They are not very rich in texture, nor can the ideas be accounted of any great significance. Nevertheless they are more contrapuntal and decorative than the early quartets of Haydn, and are not without melodic features of happy geniality. In the first of the set, in D (K. 155), for instance, we find a Finale which is founded on a theme of remarkable freshness and rustic charm :

Ex. 2.

Unfortunately the promise of this opening is not quite fulfilled, for we have, in the course of the movement,

such passages of 'padding' as the following, which
lead nowhere and are not interesting in themselves :

The second quartet of this set, in G (K. 156), opens
with a light-hearted strain which sounds more like a
Finale than a first movement, and after an expressive
Adagio in E minor, finishes with a Minuet and Trio.

The third, in C (K. 157), is rather prim and formal
throughout and presents little variety in its part-writing ;
the fourth, in F (K. 158), is even less eventful. Stronger
thematic and rhythmic interest pervades the fifth of
the group, in B flat (K. 159), particularly in an Allegro
in G minor which follows the opening Andante. There
are strange suggestions here of Mozart's later style,
particularly in the episode beginning thus :

The final Rondo, however, is in the nature of a relapse
into the square and obvious, and has some very dull
' manufactured ' episodes.

In No. 6 of this set, in E flat (K. 160), Mozart

exhibits more originality and, as regards the first movement at least, is more economical with his thematic material, and sticks to his points with infinitely greater mastery and satisfaction. The Adagio and final Presto are less important : the former is graceful, but brief and not much developed, whilst in the latter he reverts to the use of mechanical passage-work such as that which disfigures the Finale of the first D major Quartet.

This group is, however, very instructive to the student, for the quartets are structurally of progressive interest and show that the composer's powers grew as he worked, in a remarkably steady way. The next batch of Mozart's string quartets, which can again conveniently be gathered into a cluster of six (K. 168–73), appear to have been composed in quick succession during August and September 1773. Jahn tells us that they were written in Vienna, the birth-place and domain of Haydn's chamber music, and one can imagine how, as he points out, ' the ambitious youth would exert himself to satisfy the demand for the highest class of compositions ' in this great musical centre. It is interesting to note that these Vienna quartets remained unpublished for fifteen years, when, after the composer had achieved wide fame, they were brought out as ' Six Quartets by Mozart, at a low price ', with no hint of the period at which they were composed. This led to some kind of protest from the publisher of the later quartets, who evidently regarded his business rival's methods as on a par with his prices.

These quartets are certainly works of larger scope than the previous six, and, while they do not as yet exhibit the complete grace or rare beauty of form which we associate with the fully-fledged Mozart, they attempt far more in the matter of logical thematic development. Moreover the composer's inventive powers had already ripened to the extent that he was able almost entirely to dispense with passages of ' padding ' and mere note-manufacture to fill up time and space. Each of the quartets has four movements.

The opening Allegro of the first of this set, in F (K. 168), may be quoted as an early example of a method of development which became very prominent in Mozart's later work :

The third bar of this initial theme is singled out for embellishment in the 13th bar, and when the ' working-out ' section arrives it is this figure, not the whole theme, which comes forward for discussion :

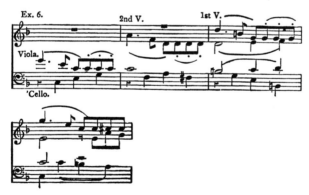

This is an early instance of a type of workmanship which Beethoven adopted with such success and which became traditional in sonata construction. Indeed, the episodical utilization of figures derived from fragments of the main theme is a device often described as a special innovation of Beethoven.

The Andante shows, perhaps for the first time in Mozart's chamber music, a real mastery of contrapuntal methods, and, incidentally, the use of mutes. The treatment of the opening phrase is in the manner of a canon :

Ex. 7.

The four parts throughout are equally interesting and important.

The Minuet is a slight but charming miniature, and discloses a dainty theme :

Ex. 8.

In the Trio, which is in the key of B flat major, there is some effective imitative writing in which all the instruments participate, as in the Andante quoted in Ex. 7.

The Finale takes the form of a strictly organized Fugue on the following lively subject :

Ex. 9.

Here we find the young composer rejoicing in his newly-found skill to construct such ingenious and effective *stretti* as the following :

Ex. 10.

and a similarly playful treatment of the theme inverted, a few bars later.

There is nothing quite so unconstrained or vivacious as this in any of the preceding quartets, but the style is a trifle monotonous and there is little in the nature of contrast, which is such a valuable device in quartet music.

In the Quartet in A (K. 169), the next of this set,

I   B

there are again some constructive features worthy of attention. In the first movement the rhythm of the concluding phrases of the ' exposition '

Ex. 11.

is seized upon after the double bar, and the brief development section is chiefly concerned with a contrapuntal discussion of this rhythm. This plan of turning what seems to be a mere chance remark in the codetta into a main topic of conversation became a very favourite method of treatment with Mozart in after years.

An Andante in D major, in the nature of a cavatina, follows. This is noteworthy for suave melody and the free use of double notes in the accompaniment :

Ex. 12.

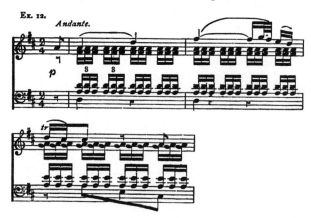

In the Minuet the delicate grace of the broken phrases

which form the opening (singularly suggestive of 'God save the King', both in melody and harmony)

Ex. 13.

seems to promise something more interesting than that which actually ensues. The Finale is called a 'Rondeau', the subject of which hops out before us in a very amusing way :

Ex. 14.   *Allegro.*

but, like most of Mozart's early Finales, it does not contain much music that calls for special comment.

The third quartet of this group (K. 170) is in C major and begins with a set of variations. It is the first of Mozart's quartets in which variations occur. The theme is somewhat reminiscent of Haydn, and begins thus :

Ex. 15.   *Andante.*

The variations are of the old-fashioned decorative kind, that is to say they are variations which simply 'vary' and do not expatiate upon the text provided by the theme. The most inventive is the last, where the quiet phrases of the melody are humorously interrupted by loud rumbling ejaculations, *tutti*, in demisemiquavers :

Ex. 16.

After this the theme is repeated, unadorned.

A Minuet and Trio, of no special moment, is succeeded by a slow movement, in G, which consists mainly of a series of melodic solo passages for 1st violin, viola, and 2nd violin in turn, simply accompanied by chords of detached quavers. Again one is reminded of Haydn.

Ex. 17.

A little Rondo, an almost trivial movement in which there is a great deal of repetition of figures of very slight importance, and little attempt to weld the ideas into a continuous whole, completes the quartet, which is perhaps rather less interesting than its companions.

The fourth quartet of the set, in E flat (K. 171), displays more invention and originality. There is a short introductory Adagio, opening with a significant unison phrase, which has a graceful corollary to round it off :

Ex. 18.

The Allegro, to which this dignified opening leads us, possesses real Mozartian charm and delicacy of fancy, as the following few bars of the main subject will show :

Ex. 19.

The easy progress of the music is only disturbed by the sudden return of the Adagio (a fine unexpected touch), which concludes the movement.

The Minuet of this quartet is remarkable in having a theme consisting of two sections of 5-bar rhythm, but the melodic interest here is not very great. An exceedingly contrapuntal, almost Bach-like, Andante

follows, and the Finale, an *Allegro assai* in sonata form,
is naïve and humorous in its main subject,

Ex. 20.

and even more delightfully merry in its chirping second
theme :

Ex. 21.

It is a pleasant movement all through, and may perhaps convey to the fancifully minded a suggestion of

> birds in the boughis sheen,
> Singing of love among the leavës small.

The fifth quartet, in B flat (K. 172), opens in the
following business-like and serviceable way—not free
from convention, but also not devoid of charm of
phrase :

Ex. 22.

The 2nd subject is a charming melody of a somewhat Tyrolean cast (it may be remembered that Mozart was born in the Austrian Tyrol, and even in a work as mature as the Clarinet Quintet the influence of Tyrolean folk-melodies comes peeping out). Following the lead of Haydn in many of his quartets he sets the melody to be played by the 1st and 2nd violins in octaves :

Ex. 23.

Upon these two themes the whole of the brief movement depends, and it never departs from the mood of formal elegance which both these subjects express. For the Adagio Mozart provides an expres-

sive solo melody for the 1st violin. It is accompanied
by constantly moving semiquavers, ingeniously dove-
tailed by the 2nd violin and viola, and the 'cello
supplies a simple succession of detached basses. The
Minuet is unusually contrapuntal in style for the period,
but there is relief in the gentle little Trio which, with
its simple detached notes and obvious rhythm, is the
most innocent thing in the world.

The Finale has a little more texture than Mozart's
Finales at this stage of his progress were wont to exhibit,
and possesses a 2nd subject which is charmingly distri-
buted between the instruments :

It is in first-movement form, but the development
section is very short and unpretentious.

The last quartet of this group, No. 6 in D minor

(K. 173), opens with a movement which has some noteworthy touches of fun. It begins seriously enough :

Ex. 25.

but on arriving, after only 16 bars, at the 2nd subject Mozart shows us that he is much more interested in what he has to say here. The quaint melody seems almost to be suggested by the sounds which emanate from a poultry run! Surely this is the clucking of many hens in different keys ?

Ex. 26.

And so it proceeds for quite a long time. After the double bar, with still greater humour, Mozart, instead of elaborating what has gone before, simplifies. Our attention is claimed by a solo hen, who begins like this and goes on cheerfully chuckling to herself for a great many bars :

Ex. 27.

It is all very amusing, and quite the best farm-yard music that has ever been composed!

A graceful Andante in D major (a somewhat unusual sequence of keys), a Minuet, as formal and stately as usual, follow, and the Finale takes the shape of a strict Fugue on a very serious chromatic subject :

This is not a theme which lends itself to much variety of treatment, but the composer succeeds, by dwelling with a good deal of persistency upon the figure of the last two beats of the third bar, in getting plenty of animation and diatonic movement into the piece. He does not miss the chances of chromatic effects, which are particularly telling in the *stretti*. But nothing he has to say in these last three movements can quite drive away the smiles excited by the first movement. We cannot forget the poultry, or our curiosity to know how Mozart was inspired to conceive such a thoroughly irresponsible and comic piece of tone-painting.

II

The Six String Quartets dedicated to Haydn

In these quartets we find Mozart's art at its ripest. After he had completed the quartets already dealt with the composer did not turn his attention to this form of writing for something like nine years. It was in 1782 that he began the sequence of six great works which must always be ranked amongst his most famous masterpieces.

The quartets may be tabulated as follows :

No. 1 in G major (K. 387), dated 31 December 1782.
No. 2 in D minor (K. 421), dated June 1783.
No. 3 in E flat major (K. 428), belonging also to 1783.
After this there was a pause in the creation of quartets, which was broken by the composition of

No. 4 in B flat major (K. 458), dated 9 November 1784,

followed by

No. 5 in A major (K. 464) and
No. 6 in C major (K. 465),

both of which were composed in January 1785.

The six quartets were published during the autumn of 1785 with a graceful dedication to Haydn, in which the composer declares that they are the fruit of long and earnest application.

These works were not received with complete approbation by the critics of the day. Even one of the most favourable expresses the opinion that ' it is a pity that in his truly artistic and beautiful compositions Mozart should carry his effort after originality too far, to the detriment of the sentiment and heart of his works. His new quartets, dedicated to Haydn, are much too highly spiced to be palatable for any length of time.' The chief bone of contention was apparently the opening of the sixth quartet, as we shall see later. In any case these severe comments are strange reading for the present generation. Mozart had passed the experimental stage. He had formed a style which must have been familiar to the whole world of music. His mastery could not be questioned. In these quartets each part has equal importance in the scheme, and the instruments are handled with an ease and freedom which no other composer of quartets ever achieved in quite the same degree.

Let us first examine in detail the opening four bars of No. 1 in G major, for they will reveal to us, in short space, that unerring perfection of musical texture which is, perhaps, analogous to what painters call 'quality'.

Ex. 29.   *Allegro vivace assai.*

This is flawless quartet writing. We can think of no other medium which could deliver the message as it is here delivered. It is not a harmonized melody : the thought itself is a four-part thought. And immediately it is expressed Mozart shows us that complete unity of action is not the only virtue his delicate machinery possesses. He has personalities to deal with—they can converse as well as blend their tones. The viola has something to say—the 2nd violin can respond by repeating the same notes with its own characteristic voice. It is left for the 1st violin to carry the phrase aloft and round it into a perfect whole.

Ex. 30.

There is, unfortunately, no space here to carry such detailed analysis further. It must suffice to say that these eight bars are quoted in score to give a clear

sample of the quality of Mozart's workmanship and
line-work throughout the movement. This subject-
matter is spun with the greatest ease into successions
of florid melodic figures, which are only interrupted
by the appearance of an engaging 2nd subject, given
out, in the first instance, by the 2nd violin :

Ex. 31.

This tune, in turn, is subjected to decorative treatment, culminating in a crisp concluding figure :

Ex. 32.

The development section is brimful of the happiest in-
genuities, the beauties of which can only be relished by
a close study of the score.   First the utmost value is ex-
tracted from the opening theme, discussed in different
keys by the three upper instruments in turn ; afterwards the last two bars of Ex. 31, as well as the delicate
rhythms of Ex. 32, are a fruitful source of inspiration
to the composer.

The writing, elaborate as it is, is always crystal-
clear, but so much is made of every detail that there
seems nothing left for the recapitulation section to
undertake other than simple restatement.   Mozart
shows his wisdom in giving the listener exactly what
his ears desire—a plain repetition which differs only

from the exposition in the necessary transposition of the 2nd subject into G major. There is no Coda.

The Minuet comes next. It is a most interesting example. Indeed Mozart offers us here an entirely unconventional view of this measure. There is nothing quite on a par with it, even in Beethoven, for expansive originality of structure. In the first two bars we are given a hint of the formal lilt. But, as Mr. H. C. Colles points out in his *Growth of Music*,[1] this is done ' of set purpose, to act as a foil to the strangely accented chromatic passages which follow on the first violin copied in contrary motion by the violoncello '. ' The charm lies ', he adds, ' in first setting a familiar pattern, then wiping it out, and finally establishing it at the cadence,' as will be shown in the following example :

Ex. 33.

An examination of the complete score will reveal, also, that the form of the movement is far more developed

[1] H. C. Colles, *The Growth of Music*, vol. ii, Chap. IV, Oxford University Press.

than usual. It is akin to that of a regular sonata movement with 2nd subject,

working-out, and recapitulation of both themes complete.

The Trio (in G minor) is shorter, and in the customary pattern, with a vigorous uprising initial theme,

in marked contrast with everything which has preceded it.

The beautifully wrought *Andante cantabile* in C
major, which forms the third movement, has also an
ascending arpeggio theme, but it is of a very different
character :

The mood is almost entirely contemplative, but the
score is full of expressive turns of phrase and rich
passages of musical embroidery. It is not a movement
which lends itself readily to textual quotation. The
following brief extract from one of its episodes must
serve as a fair example of the exquisite phraseology
which Mozart so lovingly controls :

The construction of the Finale is most unusual and most successful. The movement opens with a fugal exposition on a semibreve subject which reminds one in shape of the famous semibreve theme in the Finale of the 'Jupiter' Symphony. Here is the subject, with its answer and the counter-subject :

After the 'cello and viola have entered in turn, in regular fugal method, the music suddenly abandons its severity and breaks off into a tripping dance-tune, the setting of which is the very reverse of contrapuntal :

Ex. 39.

This is repeated, the 2nd violin becoming the soloist, after which the viola and 'cello re-echo the tail end of the phrase, which is then continued contrapuntally. A chromatic passage, supported by an inner ' pedal ' note (a repeated A on the viola), leads to a chord of A major and the arrival of the 2nd subject.   This subject is similarly divided into two sections, the first part fugal in exactly the same way as with the principal theme, but beginning this time on the 'cello :

Ex. 40.

Into the continuation of this the semibreve subject (Ex. 38) is most deftly interwoven, after which we have a solo section exactly corresponding in importance to the dance measure of Ex. 39, accompanied with simple chords and chord-figures :

A variation of this and a short codetta (all in the same graceful strain) conclude the first part of the movement. The development section opens with yet another melodic figure, a little chromatic scale-phrase

which is treated in counterpoint for 18 bars. The 1st subject (Ex. 38) then reappears, traversing an interesting series of remote keys. The recapitulation has no definite starting-point—a device which Beethoven is generally supposed to have invented—but when the dance-tune (Ex. 39) enters, transposed exactly into C major, we are conscious that the development is over. The second theme (Ex. 40) takes its customary place in the *reprise*, in the customary tonic key, and the solo section (Ex. 41) is again requisitioned (also in G major) and leads to a short Coda, in which the chromatic phrases of Ex. 42, and a *stretto* of Ex. 38, are prominent features.

The second quartet of this series, in D minor (K. 421), is one of the undisputed masterpieces of quartet literature. Its moods and colouring differ

widely from those of the work just under discussion.
All four movements are serious in character, and perhaps in only one other chamber work, the famous
Quintet for strings in G minor, does Mozart ascend to
quite the same level of sustained emotional beauty as he
reaches here. In the case of the quintet the Finale,
charming though it is, is invaded by a touch of irre-
sponsibility which somehow seems to break the spell.
This quartet, on the contrary, is all of a piece in its
unity of style, as we shall see.

The first movement is singularly concise and
economical in thematic material. According to Jahn,
it is an ' affecting expression of melancholy '. The
fine opening theme is certainly darkly serious, but it is
not gloomy, for its solemnity is tempered with grace :

Ex. 43.
Allegro moderato.

sotto voce.

Nevertheless these are bold outlines, which are accen-
tuated by the repetition an octave higher, with altered

harmonies and a full close. The continuation sustains the brave freedom and the grace, as well as the firm D minor key-sense.

The closing semiquaver figure is echoed by the three companion instruments in turn, culminating in a forceful dominant seventh chord in F major in its first inversion. Though we have, thus early, reached the key of the 2nd subject, we are kept waiting for it for some ten bars of imitative writing, dealing fancifully with relevant phrases. A full close brings us to the mood the composer wishes to establish—a mood of singular serenity and ingratiating charm :

This lovely theme is followed by a decorative variant, with triplet semiquavers, and a pointedly rhythmical cadential phrase :

The number of full closes in F major is surprising (there

are seven in all), but it is still more surprising that they
never become tiresome.   Just before the double-bar
two little codetta figures, which might escape attention, should be noted, for they assume importance in the
development :

Ex. 47.

For the working-out section, as might be expected,
Mozart seizes upon the 1st subject, which, with its
octave dip, is obviously fixed in the listener's mind,
and therefore a fit topic for discussion.   He starts off
in the key of E flat major, with the *motif* of the first
two bars of Ex. 43, reminding one of some of Beethoven's bold strokes in like situations.   At first his
treatment of the 2nd bar of this subject is somewhat
persistent, but, after a striking enharmonic modulation
to A minor, he deals with the whole phrase in a series
of dissonant imitations, starting thus :

Ex. 48.

A little later considerable play is made with a variant
of the phrase of the 3rd bar of the 1st subject, and
here it is that the figure of the codetta (Ex. 47) comes
into prominence, and is tossed about from instrument
to instrument in playful sport.   Thus we are led to
the recapitulation, which pursues a fairly normal
course.   There are, however, a few transformations.
For instance, the 2nd subject is heard in D minor, and
its decorative variant (Ex. 46) is slightly altered in
notes and given fresh rhythmic energy, after the
following fashion :

There is a Coda of six bars only, for the days of long
perorations had not yet arrived.

   The second movement is a serene piece of expression,
called by Jahn a ' consolatory ' Andante ' of a melancholy quartet ', clear in purpose, concise and very
perfect in formation.   The first half, consisting of two
repeated sections beginning and ending in F major, is
balanced by a middle section with the tonality alternating between F minor and A flat major.   The first
few bars of the principal melody establish the mood.

A good deal of attention is paid to the semiquaver
figures which begin at the end of the second bar,

figures which are utilized in both portions of the
movement.   Jahn alludes to the ' ardent longing '
which they express, and the description will serve.
The broken phrases of the F minor section maintain
the sad but serene mood of the movement :

Ex. 51.

After this theme has run its course a return is made to
the whole of the first section (unaltered), and there is
a short Coda, dealing mainly with the rising semiquavers of the opening melody.

The Minuet reverts to the earnestness of the first
movement, and is as far removed from the cheery
Minuets of Haydn as from the capricious and epi-
grammatic Scherzi of Beethoven.   Let us note the
construction of the 10-bar melody, its sequential
balance, and the unity of its rhythmical design :

Ex. 52.

After this double-bar there is more of the same
rhythm, and an extension of the sequences, with a
lovely use of chromatic melody and harmony.   The
Trio is in sharp contrast, with its continuous snap-
rhythm solo melody in D major, accompanied by the

simplest tonic and dominant harmonies played *pizzi-cato* by the under strings.

Ex. 53.

Simplicity of design is here combined with great freedom in the use of wide melodic intervals.

Ex. 54.

In the final eight bars the viola joins the 1st violin in the lower octave, but the *pizzicato* chords are continued without interruption by the 2nd violin and 'cello. It is interesting to note that Mozart's use of *pizzicato* effects in his chamber music is extremely rare ; this is, indeed, the only important passage of the kind to be found in any of the string quartets. Its very isolation gives it a specially marked prominence and glitter amongst such solemn surroundings.

The Finale (in D minor) takes the form of a set of variations on a theme, in $\frac{6}{8}$ time, which is of the rhythmic nature of a *Siciliano*, beginning thus :

Ex. 55. *Allegretto, ma non troppo.*

There are four variations, followed by a return to the theme, slightly altered and extended by way of Coda.

The first variation is mostly concerned with elabora-
tions in the 1st violin part. The second variation deals
principally with bold cross-rhythms,

alternating with busy semiquaver triplet-figures. In
the third variation prominence is accorded to the
viola line, which is treated with most enterprising
freedom and fluency, as the following short extract
will show :

Var. 4 is in D major, like a sudden burst of sunshine on a quiet landscape. The final section (D
minor again) is taken *più allegro* : the repeated semiquavers of the 1st violin in the 2nd and 3rd bars of the
theme come into prominence once more, this time as
triplets :

and great play is made with this graceful bird-like chirping right up to the closing bars of the quartet.

The third quartet of the group, in E flat (K. 428), is rich in the possession of many and varied beauties. It is less uniformly solemn than the D minor. For two movements, at least, it touches an unaccustomed note of quiet sadness and almost ethereal tranquillity, whilst the Finale transports us to fairyland. If the falling octave in a minor key expresses melancholy, the rising octave in the major betokens hope. The subject of the opening *Allegro ma non troppo* is in unison for all the instruments :

Ex. 59.

and this is followed by the soft interplay of significant phrases from the 1st and 2nd violins, still a little hushed and wrapped in mystery :

Ex. 60.

The 2nd subject, when it arrives, has definite melodic continuity, but hovers, undecided, between the keys of G minor and B flat major (Ex. 61).

The melody is subjected to repetition with the viola as spokesman. Its expansion is brief. After the double-bar we have a version in canon of the 1st subject, which is not, however, further developed. Practically

the whole of this section is concerned with a chain of
figures derived from the opening half-bar of Ex. 61—

Ex. 61.

a phrase which the key of E flat seems to render
familiar, for is not its counterpart a prominent characteristic of Beethoven's 'Emperor' Concerto? These
figures are bound together by repeated notes and
sweeping arpeggio passages in triplets,

Ex. 62.

which recur in various keys, and on every instrument
in turn. The recapitulation is quite normal, and there
is no Coda.

At the opening of the Andante Mozart seems to be
engrossed in what is commonly called a 'brown
study'. It is a mood most unusual with him. If we
look at the first six bars we shall see that this is not by
any means melody in the ordinary accepted sense.
The 'cello wanders quietly amongst its middle notes

in grave meditation—the upper parts, with their syncopations and dark low tone, are purely harmonic:

These calm reflections are not disturbed by what follows, and though the notes are transferred to higher octaves the same meditative mood prevails. Still later we have drifted into what seems like a dim dream of half-recollected sorrows,

with a responsive echo, strangely mystic in expression, and still more strangely anticipative of the opening

theme of Wagner's *Tristan und Isolde* (a coincidence
already noted by Stanford in his *Musical Composition*) :

The movement is in sonata form, and in the brief
development section the roaming 'cello quaver-shapes
of Ex. 63 are transferred to the upper voices, whilst
the accompanying syncopations become more and more
chromatic, with growing poignancy of expression. We
are thus led to a return of the first section without any
awakening from our dreams. Even Mozart, most
spiritual-minded of musicians, never conceived a more
unearthly, a more truly religious piece of music than this,
where four gently blended voices seem, as it were from a
distance, to speak ' authentic tidings of invisible things '.

We are brought into our own world again with a
jerk, by the forceful opening of the Minuet—almost
the only strongly rhythmical bars in the whole quartet :

This is breezy, vital music, relieved with touches of
pure rusticity such as the following, over a sustained
B flat harmony,

Ex. 67.

as well as by a dainty passage of detached chords which
suggests the sudden appearance of wood-nymphs upon
the scene :

Ex. 68.

The Trio is mainly in B flat major, but begins above a
low pedal C of the 'cello in the following delightful way :

Ex. 69.

It is noteworthy for its further succession of pedal-
basses, on B flat, G, F, and B flat in turn, and for the
continuity of its wavy quaver phrases.

The Finale is a Rondo, and its dainty dance-like

subject suggests that the wood-nymphs, who certainly
arrived during the progress of the Minuet, are staying
with us to trip a measure for our delight :

Ex. 70.
Allegro vivace.

In these broken phrases and in scampering semiquavers the general liveliness is continued throughout
a long subject and a modulating episode. The next
definite tune, when it comes, is a little more wistful in
style, though it by no means contradicts the animated
manner of the rest. A resemblance to Ex. 61 seems to
connect the 2nd bar of the melody with some prominent episodes in the first movement, but it is probably
an unconscious connexion.

Ex. 71.

Upon these two themes and their tributaries the whole of this very light movement is based. The Coda is irresistibly charming and ends with a suggestion of the final disappearance of the nymphs, in a passage which is worthy of Mendelssohn's fairy music at its best.

Ex. 72.

This is a bewitching ending to a work which perhaps suffers, as a whole, from excess of variety, for it covers almost too diverse a field of musical experience in the course of its four movements.

'*THE MUSICAL PILGRIM*'

General Editor   *Dr. Arthur Somervell*

MOZART'S
STRING QUARTETS

BY

THOMAS F. DUNHILL

BOOK II

GREENWOOD PRESS, PUBLISHERS
WESTPORT, CONNECTICUT

Originally published in 1927
by Oxford University Press, London

Reprinted from an original copy in the collections
of the Brooklyn Public Library

First Greenwood Reprinting 1970

Library of Congress Catalogue Card Number 77-104260

SBN 8371-3919-8

Printed in the United States of America

CONTENTS

BOOK II

II. THE SIX STRING QUARTETS DEDICATED TO
HAYDN (*continued*)

Quartet in B flat (K. 458) . . 5

Quartet in A (K. 464) . . 11

Quartet in C (K. 465) . . 16

III. THE LAST STRING QUARTETS . . 25

Quartet in D (K. 499) . . 25

Adagio and Fugue (K. 546) . . 30

Quartet in D (K. 575) . . 34

Quartet in B flat (K. 589) . . 38

Quartet in F (K. 590) . . 39

BOOK II

The Six String Quartets dedicated to Haydn (continued)

THE B flat Quartet (K. 458), which comes next in the series as No. 4, is known in Germany as the ' Jagd-Quartet ', from the character of the leading theme of the first movement, which is of the jovial ' hunting-horn ' type, and is in $\frac{6}{8}$ time, as such pieces generally are. It starts off in the most direct manner

Ex. 73.

and pursues an easy and merry course in the same vein for about forty bars, sometimes enlivened by bustling semiquaver scales. At the 26th bar the theme conveys a very definite suggestion of horns, below a trill on the 1st violin :

Ex. 74.

The key of B flat is maintained with almost dogged persistence, but eventually a quite simple modulatory passage leads to the dominant of F, when a little tag-phrase,

is immediately repeated by all the instruments separately ' with a mocking sort of air ', as Jahn says, and afterwards ' retained and treated as the germ of numerous freely developed images '. It is the basis, first of all, of what must be called the 2nd subject—which is in reality more a succession of glittering musical spangles than a definite theme. The 2nd violin leads off :

This is repeated in the upper octave by the leader, and the exposition closes with some references to sections of the hunting theme. Perhaps because he has not provided a well-defined 2nd subject, Mozart starts the development section with an entirely new 16-bar melody, beginning in F major,

and ending, unexpectedly, in F minor. Fragmentary semiquaver groups, akin to those in Ex. 75, are then resumed, and tossed from one instrument to another in sportive fashion. Eventually we return to the main subject and the recapitulation is crowned with a Coda which is exceptionally long for Mozart. It appears to have a special purpose. As if to make up for what he had failed to do in the middle of the movement, Mozart expends his energies afresh on a very systematic imitative treatment of the hunting theme, and though he never ventures to stray from the tonality of B flat, there is so much rhythmical variety that the unchanged key-colouring does not create a feeling of monotony. If there is one thing that the composers of the eighteenth century understood far better than those of the twentieth, it was how to stay in one key without weariness !

A Minuet, suave and courteous, of the true minuet character, comes next. It is not the best or most typical Mozart. The rhythmic balance of the melody, however, is interesting and a little complicated; detached phrases are grouped in a curious way, which makes the tune a little difficult to grasp as a whole.

Ex. 78.

There are no unexpected structural features. It is as short as the Minuets of the early quartets. The Trio, which remains in B flat, has a more easily felt continuity, and is in Mozart's favourite 10-bar formation.

The slow movement is the great outstanding feature of the work. It is really a slow movement—the only

actual Adagio of the six quartets—and boasts an extremely eloquent and dignified theme. Nobility of
outline is combined with rhythmic subtlety. It is an
aristocratic melody in the grand manner, but there is
no hint of pretentiousness :

Ex. 79.

After this impressive start the melody is carried aloft
by the 1st violin, and becomes at once of a richly florid
character without ever losing ' that floating Grecian
grace ', as Schumann described the lovely outlines of
Mozart's music. The movement is so continuous, and
each phrase is so dependent upon what has immediately
preceded it, that it is almost impossible to elucidate by
means of quotation. The sinuous grace of a passage
such as the following, for instance, beautiful though it
may be to contemplate in isolation, is far more satisfying amongst relevant surroundings (Ex. 80). Only
a study of the score will reveal how the composer, with
unerring art, continues this conversation between 1st
violin and 'cello, gradually adding movement to the

accompanying harmonies, until the score seems almost to tremble with demisemiquavers, and the opening theme is touched upon again, to be carried even further

Ex. 80.

aloft than before. Most of the material is, in fact, repeated a fourth higher this time, until after an interrupted cadence we have a finish which breathes the spirit of heavenly peace. Parry, whose appreciation of Mozart's music is too often lukewarm and reluctant, speaks of this conclusion as a beautiful instance of a Coda constructed out of ejaculatory fragments of the 1st subject, 'never touching its first phrase, but passing like a sweet broken reminiscence':

Ex. 81.

The Finale, reverting to the joyous gaiety of the first movement, breaks the spell. It has a subject which is almost careless in its abandonment to the obvious, and yet fascinates from the sheer audacity of saying, without shame, the first impudent thought that comes to hand :

Perhaps it was the last two bars of this which Beethoven had in his mind when he made the quaint cadence to the subject of the final movement of his G major piano Concerto—for it is a strange touch of irresponsible humour for two musicians to light upon independently. Mozart is so hugely pleased with the

little joke he has perpetrated that he repeats this
skittish phrase of five notes no less than six times in the
course of twelve bars, until it becomes a kind of catch-
word which we are ready to recognize and smile at
whenever it is uttered. The cheery score might have
been signed by Haydn himself—it is far more like
Haydn than Mozart.

It should be noted that this movement, though
sometimes described as a Rondo, is really in sonata
form. It has, however, three definite subjects instead
of the usual two. The second and third themes are
both in F major, and of equal importance. One begins
in sprightly sections, connected by a little feathery
scale-phrase for the 1st violin :

the other provides the only episode of quiet sustained
writing in the movement, and thus affords a much-
needed moment of comparative repose :

The development section is occupied entirely with a
spirited treatment of the 1st subject, and the recapitulation reproduces all three subjects in the tonic key,
without deviation from conventional methods.

The Quartet in A, No. 5 of the set (K. 464), is un-
doubtedly, to modern ears, a less arresting and a less
eventful work than any of its five companions. It is
certainly not popular with present-day string players,

and is seldom performed in public. Why ? The work
has a quiet graciousness all its own, and, if its sentiment
never runs very deep, there is no lack of that polished
phraseology and fluent inevitable part-writing which
distinguishes Mozart's music at its best. The style,
however, is particularly reticent, and the expenditure
of thematic material particularly economical. It is
also, perhaps, rather less individual than usual, and
more continuously expressive of that ' disinterested-
ness ' which a French writer has declared to be the
cardinal quality of Mozart's most typical compositions.

The first movement of the quartet is almost entirely
suave and flowing, and is easy to listen to from the
opening bars :

Ex. 85.

This engaging phrase is repeated a degree lower in the
scale, followed by another sequential passage, *f*, and
in unison for all four instruments :

Ex. 86.

The progress towards the 2nd subject has some unusual harmonic features. The dominant chord of
E major is reached through an extension of the main
theme in the key of C, a 6–3 chord on C, and an aug-
mented 6th chord on C. We are then ready for the
new theme, which is again graceful in character, but
enlivened with bright running triplet groups :

Ex. 87.

The exposition is short; the development (in comparison) is rather long; it deals principally with the 1st subject and its corollary, Ex. 86.

The second movement consists of an Andante with variations. The theme, in D major, is melodious without being specially distinguished. The first half is as follows:

Ex. 88.

The variations are rather elaborately wrought. This is the only movement of the quartet which deals with any complexities of texture, and it is lengthy in proportion with the rest of the work, especially if the repeat-marks are observed. Mozart's aim has evidently been to give all the players enterprising passages to play. Points worthy of note are the florid decorations of the 1st violin in Var. 1, the deft use of undulating triplet semiquavers in a beautiful D minor variation, and the extended developments embarked upon in a most effective Finale which is built almost entirely upon a springing bass of march-like rhythm:

Ex. 89.

The Minuet, like the opening Allegro, is based upon two little melodic sequences, one upward, the other downward :

Ex. 90.

The merit of these phrases is the ease with which they can be combined together, as the succeeding four bars will show :

Ex. 91.

They are also treated by inversion and in canon. The whole of the Minuet is based upon such ingenious combinations, which are manipulated with extraordinary facility. The Trio, in E major, derived from the following melody, set above a descending 'cello scale, is delightful :

Ex. 92.

The rhythm of the 3rd bar comes in for some discussion by the 2nd violin, below some free triplet quavers, and much use is made of scale movement, both in crotchets and quavers.

In the Finale we once again have a theme founded on sequences, which begins with one of those little chromatic figures from which Mozart is always able to extract every ounce of meaning :

Ex. 93.

The construction of the movement is curious. It is in sonata form, but the 2nd subject is practically the same as the 1st, transposed to E major and turned into a kind of canon above a tonic pedal :

Ex. 94.

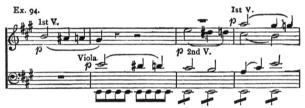

There is consequently only one main idea, and variants of it occupy most of the development, although in that section the continuity is interrupted, most happily, by a beautiful chorale-like theme in D major, which (except for two chromatic bars) is not apparently derived from anything which has previously been heard :

Ex. 95.

The Chorale is continued with flowing semiquaver embroideries on the 2nd violin, and we are soon led back to the 1st subject. After the usual recapitulation there is a Coda, still expatiating upon Ex. 93, and this effectively written, but rather unvaried Finale ends with a cadence which once more faintly whispers the oft-repeated text of the composer's discourse :

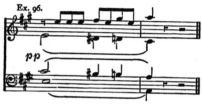

Ex. 96.

The Quartet in C (K. 465), the last of the six dedicated to Haydn, opens with the mystical Adagio introduction which is not only memorable for its anticipation of modern chromaticism but famous for the remarkable stir that it created at the time of its first appearance. Perhaps never in musical history has so great a fuss been made about so few bars of music.

The chief offence against convention was the audacity of the ' false-relations ', which, however, were as naught in comparison with those which old William Byrd had perpetrated in England more than two centuries earlier, and which had been accepted with little question by an unsophisticated and less rule-ridden generation. However, the authorities in 1785 decreed that Mozart was guilty of an offence against good sense and good taste, of, as some believed, had allowed the parts to be issued full of mistakes. A few patrons even returned them to the publishers for the printers' errors to be remedied ! But Mozart and the engravers were right, and public opinion was wrong.

The worst of controversy of this kind is that it makes it difficult for musicians, even a century and a half later, to view the matter quite dispassionately, and to judge the offending passage purely on its merits. Here are the opening bars :

Ex. 97.

Even in these days, when 'false relations' are as plentiful in music as ripe blackberries in September, and often as succulent, the slightly acid effect of the A natural with which the 1st violin enters in the 2nd bar, and the similarly placed G natural in the 6th bar, convey a certain feeling of strangeness. The other deviations from orthodoxy, over which the pedants of the day shook their hoary heads, are, however, less apparent to us in sound than on paper, and we can easily realize, as Haydn said, that if Mozart wrote them 'he had a good reason for it'. That good reason was obviously the spirit of questioning which he wished to express at the moment, and it is not likely that either conformity or non-conformity to technical rules entered into his calculations. The mood lasts for fifteen bars. There is then a prolonged resting-point on a clear dominant basis—six bars and a pause—which prepares the mind for the Allegro. This discloses a long shapely tune, which is plain sailing after what has gone before, though it is obviously full of possibilities :

Ex. 98.

Imitative treatment of the opening bars, and some bustling semiquaver figures, usher in a lively 2nd subject :

Ex. 99.

There is some free play with the broken-third passage of the 2nd bar before a 3rd subject of equal importance appears :

Ex. 100.

The doubling of this melody in the tenth below on the 2nd violin is a charming device, and the chromatic counterpoint which is woven beneath the latter half of the above phrase is exquisitely wrought. Development of the 1st subject is embarked upon sixteen bars before the double bar, as if the composer were impatient to show what he could do with a fruitful theme before the appointed time. He has, however, a large fund of inventiveness in reserve. Jahn's opinion that in Mozart's first movements the centre of gravity is always to be found in the working-out portion is nowhere better justified than in this particular instance. The energy is splendidly sustained : for forty-eight bars the music moves from strength to strength with unflagging rhythmical resource. The opening phrase of the 1st subject is the chief fount of inspiration. Not only does it appear in its original shape, but it is the rhythmical parent of a long sequence of fine imitative passages, of which the following is a good example :

Ex. 101.

Recapitulation presents no unusual features, but there is a Coda of considerable importance, and a beautiful *pp* close on a tonic pedal.

The Allegro is followed by an Andante cantabile of exceptionally tender expressiveness—possibly the most emotionally satisfying slow movement from any of Mozart's quartets. It opens with a queenly melody :

Ex. 102.

An episode, in which a most intriguing little curly figure of four notes

Ex. 103.

is dealt with conversationally, by 1st violin and 'cello in turn, leads to a second theme, fully as expressive as the first, which climbs upward over a wavy bass and is very noteworthy for the colouring resulting from the free crossing of the parts :

Ex. 104.

Upon these three ideas the whole fabric is built up, until, at the Coda, a new song of calm, almost holy beauty is sung by the 1st violin :

Ex. 105.

The enchantment of its setting is indescribable ; between melody and bass there is a throbbing line of semiquavers over and under which the curling repetitions of Ex. 102 continuously emerge with gentle insistence. Jahn has described this Andante as music which ' soars aloft into a region of blessedness where suffering and passion are transfigured ', a species of verbal rapturizing which, for once, seems fully justified.

The Minuet is, in its way, almost as striking, and comes before us with a confident air which is particularly manly after the somewhat feminine sensitiveness of the preceding movement (Ex. 106). The alternation of *p* and *f* phrases continues throughout the Minuet. The graceful shape of the opening quavers, the repeated chords, the striding unison passage, each and all form fruitful topics for the masterly discussion

Ex. 106.

which ensues, and there is, in addition, a delicately poised cadential phrase which will not escape attention :

Ex. 107.

The Trio, in C minor, also owes much of its effect to its charm of phrasing and dynamic contrasts, as well as to the free use of wide melodic intervals :

Ex. 108.

The accompanying figures, so daintily bowed, which bind the phrases together should also be recognized for their delicate value in the general design.

The Finale is one of those movements in which certain characteristics of Rondo form are combined with the more interesting and important features of first-movement construction—a favourite procedure with Mozart. The principal subject, cheerful though it is, has none of the gaiety or flippancy of the Finale of the B flat Quartet (K. 458), which it somewhat resembles in formation :

Ex. 109.

The first three notes of this tune are the mainspring of much that is to come; sometimes they are used as forceful ejaculations, sometimes as gentle commentaries upon what is proceeding in other directions. They are also used to start the 2nd subject, which begins as a little duet for the two violins :

Ex. 110.

A new feature is here introduced in the falling fifths which are added to the ubiquitous repeated notes. This feature becomes very important later on. A 3rd subject—and a very serious one—suddenly appears at the conclusion of a rapid torrent of semiquavers. It is in E flat major, and quite unprepared for by modulation.

Ex. 111.

It hovers for a few moments like a little cloud—

> A frown upon the atmosphere
> Which hath no business to appear,

but is dispelled by a flight of semiquavers and a resumption of the sky-blue clarity of G major, which prevails till the double bar. The development is brief but crammed full of eagerness and good things. First we have the main theme transposed to C minor, followed by a kaleidoscopic series of swift transitions through astonishingly remote keys. The score bristles with sharps and flats in close proximity. A return to C major brings with it the entry into the recapitulation section. This is normal except for a very considerable extension of the third theme, Ex. 111, which appears first in the key of A flat and is then treated, most effectively, in canon between the 'cello and 1st violin, in D flat. The Coda is tremendously vivacious, and ends with a veritable carnival of those falling fifths from Ex. 110, which sparkle like firework-stars up to the very last note of the music.

III

The Last String Quartets

THE reception accorded to the six great quartets which have just been discussed was evidently not sufficiently encouraging to Mozart to induce him to compose more works in the same form for some little time to come. Not until August 1786 did he resume his interest in quartet writing. He then wrote the single work in D major (K. 499). It has been said that in this quartet there ' may be traced an attempt to meet the taste of the public without sacrificing the dignity of the quartet style '. It is difficult to find a reason for thus attributing a conciliatory attitude to the composer in this instance, but the statement, appearing in Jahn's biography, has been widely repeated as authoritative, and is generally to be found in descriptions of this quartet by other writers.

Like Beethoven's F minor, Op. 95, it stands isolated from its fellows, and possesses some characteristics which distinguish it from the other quartets of Mozart in style. It is an optimistic work, sounding a note of earnestness in all its movements, but never touching our hearts with the revelations of deep feeling to which the finest pages of the quartets dedicated to Haydn give utterance.

The opening Allegretto is based upon a unison theme of purely chordal construction, the effect of which is derived from precision of rhythm and phrasing rather than from melodic outline :

Ex. 112.

Allegretto.

The last six beats of this are repeated on differing degrees of the scale and, after a cadence, there is some dallying with a combination of the slurred phrases and the dotted-note figure, the instruments dividing themselves up into pairs. A new and more forceful theme beginning in B minor then claims attention :

Ex. 113.

The tonality is undecided for a time, but a version of the first theme in E major leads to what must, presumably, be regarded as the proper 2nd subject, beginning with a confident and rather valiant gesture on the part of the 1st violin, strongly supported by the concurrence of the 'cello :

Ex. 114.

Our sojourn in the key of A is very soon terminated. A phrase or two in F sharp minor, immediately followed by some new matter in F major, gives us a sense of restlessness and insecure tonality which is very rare in Mozart. As we near the double bar, however, things become more settled, and a new theme, noteworthy for its dependence upon falling sixths and a pronounced ' Scotch-snap ' rhythm, is repeated several times :

Ex. 115.

The development section is very short and concerned solely with the 1st subject. This passes through several keys and is inverted, and there is an unceasing scintillation of staccato quavers in sixths, thirds, and tenths (derived from the final bars of the exposition) to accompany its progress.

Recapitulation presents no irregular features, and a short Coda deals lightly and cheerfully with the 1st subject and the afore-mentioned staccato quaver figures.

The next movement is one of Mozart's happiest and most crisply concise Minuets, with an absolutely formal but very aristocratic melody :

Ex. 116.
Allegretto.

The Trio, in D minor, is equally courtly, but its busy triplet shapes, seldom absent from the score, give it an air of superior animation :

Ex. 117.

It may be noted, in passing, that there is no resting-point at the conclusion of the Trio, for a second-time bar leads without break to the repeat of the Minuet. This became an habitual process later on with Beethoven and Schubert, but it is seldom to be found in Mozart, and it is difficult to cite a similar example, off-hand, from his works.

An Adagio follows, notable for chaste perfection of outline rather than warmth of expression. It is indeed a somewhat prim movement, with a theme which, in itself, suggests a curtsey :

Ex. 118.
Adagio.

The development of this theme seldom seeks to disturb its normal placidity. There are one or two short-lived episodes of momentary forcefulness, but in the main Mozart is content to pursue a straight course of conventional pattern-making, binding each section into a larger design which, thus framed, expresses perfect decorative beauty but little emotional significance.

The Finale deals largely with broken phrases which at the outset, since the Adagio ended in G major, seem to be still in the same key as that which has gone before :

Ex. 119.

This opening gives promise of some rather roguish merry-making. There is something of the gay humour of Papageno both here and later. Is it possible that *Die Zauberflöte*, written a few years afterwards, was already simmering in Mozart's mind when he wrote this genial Rondo? After the triplet figures have flourished for some forty bars there is an almost comic *pp* pause, and, still in the key of D, the two violins embark upon something new and equally cheery. ·This is the gist of what they have to say, and they say it twice over, above a repeated tonic pedal note on the 'cello :

Ex. 120.

We may note how the viola rather rudely interrupts them each time, and how, when the repetition is over, the spirit of Papageno seems to appear once more in a new guise :

Ex. 121.

This is a sportive phrase which demands our attention, and gains it by many repetitions, so that we are ready to recognize the outline when it appears later on in combination with the triplets of the 1st subject. The last two bars, especially, are much thrust into prominence.

There is only one other thematic fragment to which attention need be called, and that is a climbing succession of triplets in which the 'cello asserts its importance :

Ex. 122.

With these jolly little scraps of fun—one cannot better describe them—Mozart has built up one of his most bracing and breezy movements. If this was 'an attempt to meet the public taste' one is glad that the public taste was so highly rated by the composer. One hopes, also, that his public was sensible enough to realize its good fortune in possessing a writer who could enshrine the spirit of impish comedy in the purest of all art-forms without the slightest sacrifice of dignity or constructive skill.

Three years elapsed before Mozart composed full-length quartets again. Before these are discussed, however, there is one serious work for the same combination which is worthy of more than passing mention at this juncture—his Adagio and Fugue in C minor for String Quartet (K. 546), produced in June 1788. This splendid composition was, in part, an adaptation of a former work, the Fugue having been originally conceived and published for two pianofortes. It is interesting to recall that in its original form this Fugue so impressed Beethoven that he copied it out in score—a score which is still in existence in manuscript.

When Mozart re-wrote his Fugue for string quartet he added an important introductory Adagio of very great dignity and impressiveness. The opening is remarkably fine :

Ex. 123.

The writing for the strings, after this forcible beginning, becomes extraordinarily sensitive, and towards the close an enharmonic modulation, from F minor through A minor to the dominant of C, is so lovely that one is tempted to quote it in full—if for no other reasons than that the work is quite unknown to most musicians, even to those who are particular admirers of Mozart, and that the score is not easily accessible.

Ex. 124.

As Jahn says, the ' remarkable effects of suspense and
climax ' here tune the mind to ' a pitch of longing and
melancholy which makes the entry of the Fugue a
positive relief and stimulant '.   Here is the magnifi-
cently defiant subject of the Fugue, given out by the
'cello :

Ex. 125.
Allegro.

That the influence of Bach is paramount is evident
from a mere glance at the notes, and not only in the
main theme is this influence felt but in the freedom
and rhythmical independence of the counter-subject
(bars 4 to 6 of the 'cello part). We know from Jahn's
biography that at this particular period Mozart was
greatly impressed by Bach's forty-eight Preludes and
Fugues, which he was studying deeply, and that he
made arrangements of at least five of the Fugues for
string quartet. That he desired to follow in the foot-
steps of his great predecessor is clear from the style
of many of his works at this time. In skill of working-
out this quartet-fugue seems at every point fully equal
to Bach at his best. Mozart when writing in a strict
contrapuntal style, however, was inclined to severity of
manner, so that his works in the fugal form are often
less genial and less varied than those of his model.
Outside this style he delighted, as we know, in a light-
ness and delicacy of texture which Bach would probably have considered mere musical frivolity, but as
a contrapuntist Mozart takes himself and his responsi-
bilities very seriously indeed. He dons his thinking-
cap and becomes a little too self-conscious. Nevertheless this Fugue is developed at considerable length
with unfailing resourcefulness in every bar. The *stretti*

alone are remarkable : the subject is used by inversion,
in combination with itself, with the greatest ease.
Moreover, the work shows no trace whatever of having
once been a piano piece. It is not so much an arrange-
ment as a reconception. It is as fine a piece of pure
string-quartet writing as even Mozart has to show.

The three Quartets composed by Mozart in 1789
and 1790 were destined to be his last works in that
form. The charge levelled against the Quartet in
D (K. 499) might far more aptly be brought forward
in connexion with these compositions, which were
most certainly written with the object of pleasing, not
perhaps the general public, but somebody other than
the composer himself. Whilst staying in Berlin and
Potsdam early in 1789 Mozart attended many of the
private concerts given by Frederick William II, King
of Prussia. This monarch was an enthusiastic violon-
cellist, and commissioned Mozart to write some string
quartets for him (as he had previously requisitioned the
talents of Haydn and Boccherini in a similar way).
In June of 1789 the composer completed the first of his
quartets for the king, the work in D major (K. 575) ; a
year later he contributed two more for the same patron,
those in B flat major (K. 589) and F major (K. 590).
We know that at this period of his career Mozart
was almost overwhelmed with cares and sorrows, and
afflicted with great poverty. He was grateful for the
king's gift—100 Friedrichs d'or—and his promise of
further remuneration on the completion of the
quartets, and he set to work with a will. But the task
did not prove easy, and it was painful effort to complete the scores. In the circumstances it is surprising
how little one is conscious of this effort in listening to

the music. At moments, maybe, there are traces of
a lack of that spontaneity and facility which hitherto
seemed characteristic of Mozart at all times. Emotionally the quartets are on a far lower plane than
any of the six works dedicated to Haydn, and the
quality of most of the themes is decidedly inferior to
those of the D major Quartet discussed earlier in this
chapter. There is less sustained thought, and the
developments give nothing like the former display of
contrapuntal ingenuity. The subjects, indeed, seem
hardly strong enough to be capable of such treatment,
and Mozart evidently knew it, for over and over again
he seeks to hide their weakness by side-tracking and
avoiding the awkward issues.

The peculiar characteristic that compels attention,
and places these quartets in a different category from
all others, is the exceptional prominence of the violoncello parts. Mozart evidently set to work with one
great object constantly in view—to please the royal
'cellist by giving him plenty of grateful solo passages to
play, with frequent opportunities for showing off his
A string. In some of the movements all the principal
melodies are given to the 'cello, which virtually usurps
the place of the usual leader. Even the choice of keys
is obviously determined by the desire to give prominence to this one instrument, and there is no question
that such a form of preferential treatment, though
interesting as an experiment, is injurious to the
character of the works as ensemble music. The close
study of these quartets will, however, be of great value
to composition students, for the management of an
accompaniment to high solo 'cello passages is one of
the most difficult problems that a composer of string
quartets has to grapple with. One need hardly say

that Mozart's technical artistry in such situations is never at fault, and that the solutions he offers are always finely balanced and musically effective.

In what attempts to be a proportionate estimate of Mozart's quartets it is desirable not to go astray by giving too much space to a discussion of works which exhibit an unfortunate decline in musical inventiveness as well as certain retrograde tendencies. These quartets, in any case, do not call for detailed analysis, although one would gladly dwell upon certain happy features which show that the composer's inspiration had not entirely deserted him.

The first movement of the first quartet (in D, K. 575) has a square and rather ordinary principal theme, but the opening of the 2nd subject may be profitably examined for its apt method of lightly accompanying a 'cello melody :

Ex. 126.

The Andante, for which the composer has chosen the key of A (a most unusual relationship), has a flowing theme which dwells somewhat too insistently on the mediant note, and some melodic passages for the 'cello, which soar as high as the C sharp on the third space of the treble clef—a rather rarefied altitude in those days.

The subject of the Minuet, knowing what Mozart had done before in this form, is almost tame and trite, though he could not help shaping his phrases so gracefully that the essential weakness is disguised. In the Trio the 'cellist, who has been a little in the background during the Minuet, is placated by being given a long and very effective tune to perform. He is also privileged to lead off the Finale, with a theme which starts with the same notes as the principal subject of the first movement, cast in a different rhythm, the viola supplying the only accompaniment :

Ex. 127.

In many ways this is the most completely satisfying movement of the quartet. It is in Rondo form, and is for the most part designed diatonically on the broadest lines. Such a quietly joyous subject as this secondary theme, for instance, comes upon us like a breath of fresh sea-air : it is so spaciously laid out, so suggestive of sunshine and a clear sky :

Ex. 128.

The B flat Quartet (K. 589) has a first movement which starts with a rather slender principal theme, of minuet-like character, and in 6-bar rhythm :

Ex. 129.

Very soon the 'cellist is again brought into the lime-light to announce, the opening phrases of a conventional 2nd subject, and to execute chains of florid solo passages, lightly accompanied and never obscured. The development section is very loosely put together and has little progressive interest. The Larghetto which follows has yet another high 'cello melody for its principal material. It is a facile piece of music, but somewhat artificial, making much play of scale passages, both for melodic figuration and accompaniment.

The Minuet presents no special features of interest, but the Trio, in E flat, is noteworthy for its skilful lay-out of a busy accompaniment (a blend of staccato quavers and semiquavers) to a cheerful bird-like theme :

Ex. 130.

The Finale, quite a captivating little Rondo, slightly recalls the mood of the first movement of the other B flat Quartet (K. 453), but will not bear comparison with it, either as regards freshness of invention or skill in presentation. There is a pleasant suggestion of

cherubic innocence in its main theme, however, which
lingers in the memory :

Ex. 131.
Allegro assai.
1st & 2nd V.

Viola.

It is quite a short movement which does not outstay
its welcome, and there are some effective little touches
in the progress of its brief career. One in particular
should be cited—a sudden plunge into D flat major
for the second appearance of the principal subject,
a device which adds a touch of colour to the surroundings and averts all chances of monotony.

The last quartet (K. 590) of this rather pathetic
sequence of three is in the key of F, and holds, perhaps,
a rather less distinguished place amongst Mozart's works
than the previous two. The first movement has a subject which, for Mozart, is decidedly poor and lacking
in distinction.

Ex. 132.
Allegro moderato.

Much use is made of repeated-note accompaniment
when the 'cello takes up the theme on its own later
on. The old inventiveness and love of adventure
seem certainly to have deserted the composer here,

and even the little phrase at (*a*), from which one expects much, is rather dully dealt with. He is attempting to make bricks without straw—even without clay.

The Andante, in C, which follows has even less interest, and after the statement of a somewhat colourless melody, rather stiffly harmonized,

Ex. 133.
Andante.

the composer is principally concerned with semi-quaver decorations of a quite primitively conventional type. The 'cello again has a great deal to say, but nowhere is there anything much beyond complacent pattern-making for its own sake.

The Minuet is interesting rhythmically, the chief subject being in two sections each of 7-bar rhythm. The first section is as follows :

Ex. 134.

Neither here nor in the Finale is there any special prominence of the 'cello part. The composer seems to have forgotten his royal patron and become more interested in the music. The Finale, indeed, is a notable awakening. Without being one of Mozart's best movements it is easily the most fertile as well as the most charming section of this particular work. The playful opening by the 1st violin seems suddenly to have recaptured some of the composer's first youth :

Ex. 135.

After eight bars the viola takes up the strain, and there is a little contest for supremacy, 1st violin and viola continuing to vie with one another for pride of place for some time. The running semiquavers still occupy a place (in the background, however) when the charming 2nd subject arrives, and here is certainly a sign that Mozart's freshness of invention had not deserted him :

Ex. 136.

This has real freedom and resiliency as well as simple grace. There is a flash of the old brilliance, too, just after the double-bar. The first part ends, as usual, with a cadence in the dominant (C major), after which, with no preparation, there is a magic touch. The three lower strings dive down to a chord of D flat major, which is held in position while the 1st violin executes an enterprising variant of the glittering semiquaver figures already mentioned. If this had occurred in a work by Beethoven, reams would have been written by commentators about it ; hidden away in one of Mozart's least-known and most unfortunate quartets, it has quite escaped notice.

The sequence of keys which follows this effective stroke will be found to be a bold one. The semiquaver patterns are imitated at closer distances and are varied by widespread arpeggio groupings. It is all tremendously alive. After a regular, normal recapitulation there is a Coda which is extraordinarily full-toned and vivid and modern in sound for Mozart. Certain bars of it might almost be by Brahms in his most Hungarian mood, for after a bustling *fugato* passage, in which scraps of the subject are played against each other by inversion, we reach :

And so on, without loss of energy, to the appointed
finish. There are surprising things here. The bravery
of the *sf* chords in the first four bars, the restless
syncopation of the viola coupled with the rhythmic
insistence of the 2nd violin later on, and the effect of
the harsh soft harmony and wide distribution of parts
in the last two bars quoted—all these are points to be
noted with admiration.

One is glad that Mozart's last quartet, which began
so poorly, should end with an energetic outburst
which proves that the old fire could still be kindled, and
that his genius was not wholly crushed by bodily
weariness and the sorrows of the spirit which weighed
so heavily upon him.